SCHOLASTIC

CLOSE READING

NON-FICTION

AGES 7+

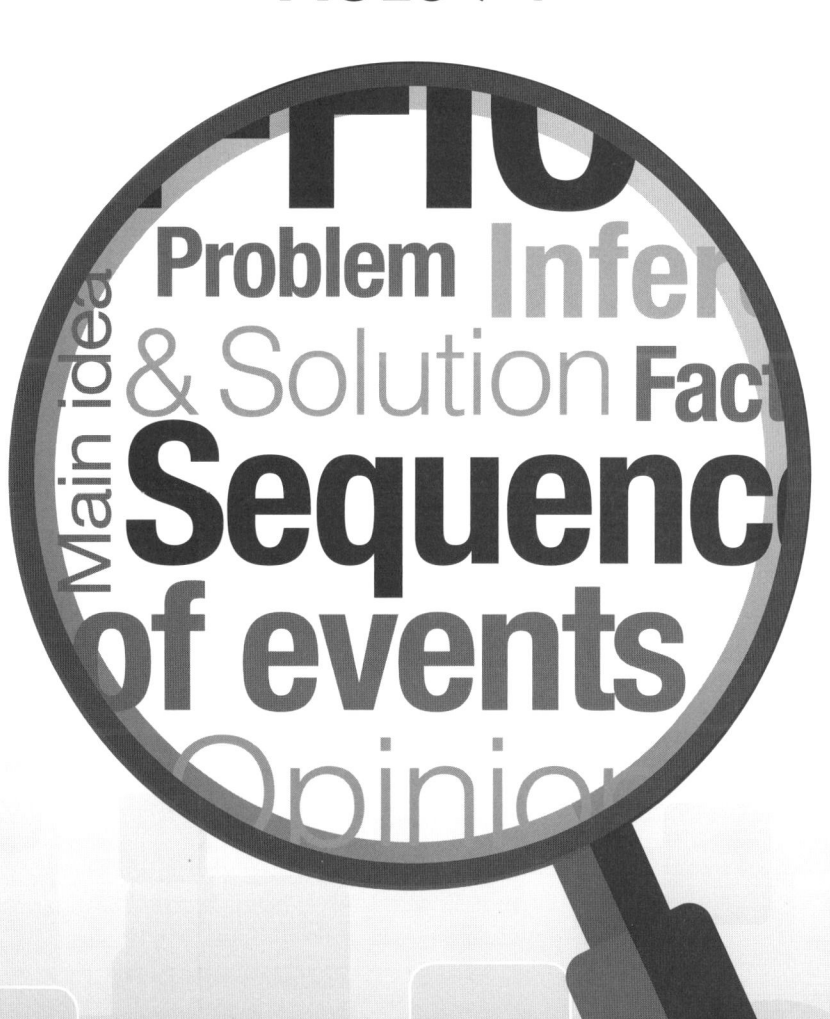

Scholastic Education, an imprint of Scholastic Ltd
Book End, Range Road, Witney, Oxfordshire, OX29 0YD
Registered office: Westfield Road, Southam, Warwickshire CV47 0RA
www.scholastic.co.uk
© 2015, Scholastic Inc. © 2019, Scholastic Ltd
123456789 9012345678

British Library Cataloguing-in-Publication Data
A catalogue record for this book is available from the British Library.
ISBN 978-1407-18282-7

Printed and bound by Ashford Colour Press

All rights reserved. This book is sold subject to the condition that it shall not, by way of trade or otherwise, be lent, hired out or otherwise circulated without the publisher's prior consent in any form of binding or cover other than that in which it is published and without a similar condition, including this condition, being imposed upon the subsequent purchaser.

No part of this publication may be reproduced, stored in a retrieval system, or transmitted, in any form or by any means, electronic, mechanical, photocopying, recording or otherwise, other than for the purposes described in the content of this product, without the prior permission of the publisher. This product remains in copyright. Every effort has been made to trace copyright holders for the works reproduced in this book, and the publishers apologise for any inadvertent omissions.

Author
Marcia Miller, Martin Lee
Editorial
Rachel Morgan, Louise Titley, Jane Wood and Rebecca Rothwell
Cover and Series Design
Scholastic Design Team: Nicolle Thomas, Neil Salt and Alice Duggan
Photographs
14: IndustryAndTravel/Shutterstock.com; 16: JeniFoto/Shutterstock.com; 18 (giant anteater): Joe McDonald/Shutterstock.com; 18 (anteater tongue): Esdeem/Shutterstock.com; 20: Jacek Chabraszewski/Shutterstock.com; 22: Kathy Massaro/Scholastic Inc; 24: Vivienstock/Shutterstock.com; 26: Anderson Press/Penguin Random House; 28: Brent Hofacker/Shutterstock.com; 30: Zynatis/Shutterstock.com; 32 (hamster): Igor Kovalchuk/Shutterstock.com; 32 (gerbil): Gelpi/Shutterstock.com; 34 (football): irin-k/Shutterstock.com; 34 (netball): xshot/Shutterstock.com; 36 (nails): Jiri Hera/Shutterstock.com; 36 (screws): Karramba Production/Shutterstock.com; 38: Magic Mine/Shutterstock.com; 40: Garry Gay/Alamy Stock Photo; 42: paylessimages/istockphoto; 44: Pete Pahham/Shutterstock.com; 46: roundstripe/Shutterstock.com; 50: Elena Dijour/Shutterstock.com; 52: Ivanastar/istockphoto

UK Revised Edition. Originally published by Scholastic Inc, 557 Broadway, New York, NY 10012 (ISBN: 978-0545-79377-3)

Contents

Introduction 5

National Curriculum Correlation 8

Teaching Routine for Close Reading and Text Marking 9

Comprehension Skill Summary Cards 11

Texts and Questions

Main Idea & Details

1	**Water All Around** (340L)	Geography Essay	14
2	**A Gifted Child** (540L)	Biographical Sketch	16
3	**No Teeth? No Problem!** (520L)	Nature Article	18

Sequence of Events

4	**A New Book** (500L)	Books Article	20
5	**Red, White and Blue** (470L)	Cooking Article	22
6	**Teach a Dog a Trick** (440L)	Training Article	24

Fact & Opinion

7	**About a Film** (560L)	Film Review	26
8	**Fajitas** (580L)	Food Essay	28
9	**Help Our Playgrounds** (550L)	Letter to the Editor	30

Compare & Contrast

10	**Hamster or Gerbil?** (490L)	Science Article	32
11	**Football and Netball** (530L)	Sports Article	34
12	**Nails and Screws** (500L)	Building Essay	36

Cause & Effect

13	**A Twitchy Muscle** (520L)	Biology Article	38
14	**Earthquake!** (530L)	Current Events Article	40

Context Clues

15	*Gyotaku* (490L)	Art History Essay	42
16	**A Musical Shape** (630L)	Music Essay	44

Problem & Solution

17	**Survival Hero** (470L)	News Article	46
18	**Bad Timing** (540L)	Business Letter	48

Summarise

19	**A Sweets Story** (520L)	History Article	50
20	**Hopi *Kachinas*** (710L)	Cultural Essay	52

Answers 54

Introduction

Texts For Close Reading and Deep Comprehension

Close reading involves careful study of a short text passage to build a deep, critical understanding of the text. By developing children's comprehension and higher-order thinking skills, you can help them make sense of the world.

> "A significant body of research links the close reading of complex text – whether the student is a struggling reader or advanced – to significant gains in reading proficiency, and finds close reading to be a key component of college and career readiness."
> (Partnership for Assessment of Readiness for College and Careers, 2012, p7)

Reading and Re-Reading For Different Purposes

The texts in *Close Reading* are carefully selected and deliberately short. This focuses children on purposeful reading, re-reading and responding. They learn about the topic through rich vocabulary development and deep comprehension.

Children re-read and analyse the text through questioning to explore:

- text structure and features
- key ideas and details
- connections/conclusions
- predictions/inferences
- words and phrases in context.

Children actively respond to the text using:

- higher-order thinking skills
- paired discussion
- written responses.

Text Marking: A Powerful Active-Reading Strategy

To improve their comprehension of informational texts, children must actively engage with the material. Careful and consistent text marking by hand is one valuable way to accomplish this. The true goal of teaching text marking is to help children internalise an effective close-reading strategy, not to have them show how many marks they can make on a page. Text-marking skills are encouraged in each passage.

Introduction

About the Texts and Questions

This book provides 20 reproducible texts that address eight key reading-comprehension skills:
- Main Idea & Detail
- Sequence of Events
- Fact & Opinion
- Compare & Contrast
- Cause & Effect
- Context Clues
- Problem & Solution
- Summarise

The contents pages detail the skills and genres covered as well as the Lexile score (see page 7). The passages are organised to help scaffold young children's understanding of each comprehension skill. Until your children are reading independently, the passages will work best as shared-reading activities or during guided reading so that you can scaffold and support readers. (See page 9 for a close-reading routine to model.)

Following each passage is a reproducible 'Questions' page of text-dependent comprehension questions.

Answers are provided. They include sample text marking and answers. Encourage children to self-assess and revise their answers as you review the text markings together. This approach encourages discussion, comparison, extension, reinforcement and correlation to other reading skills.

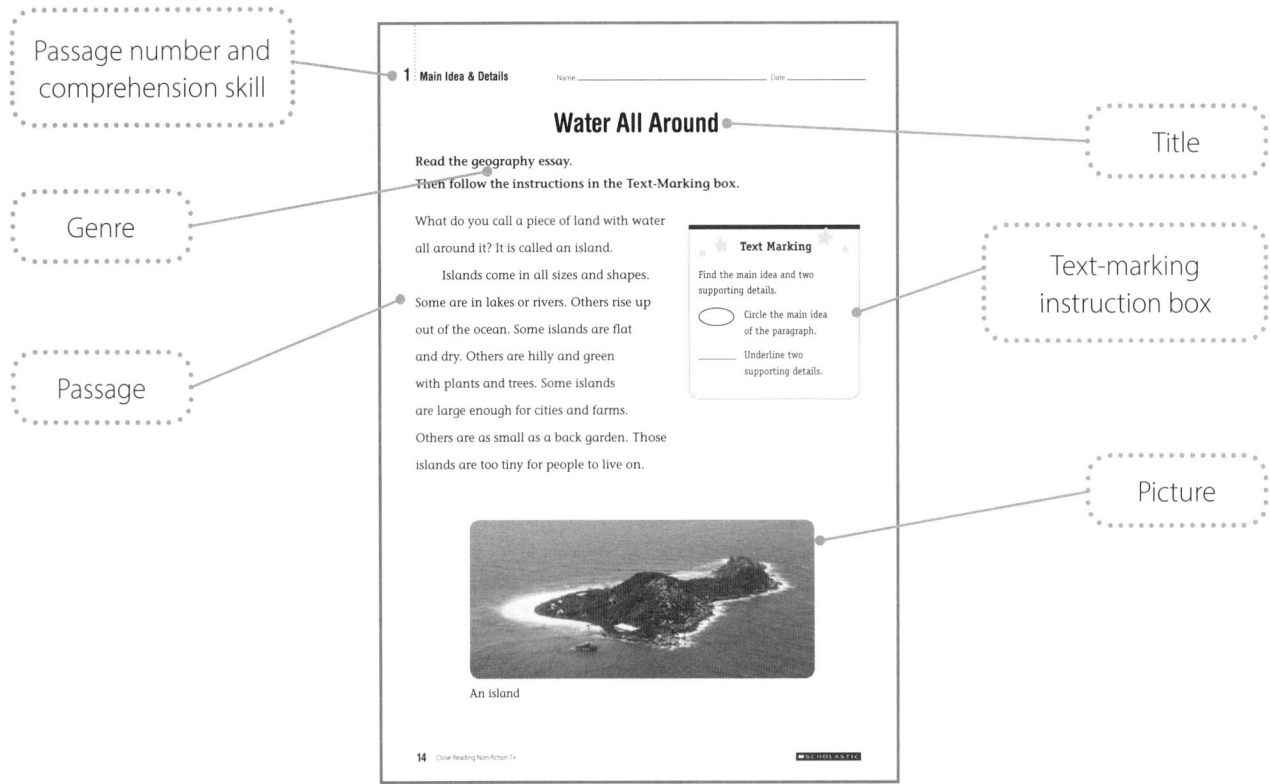

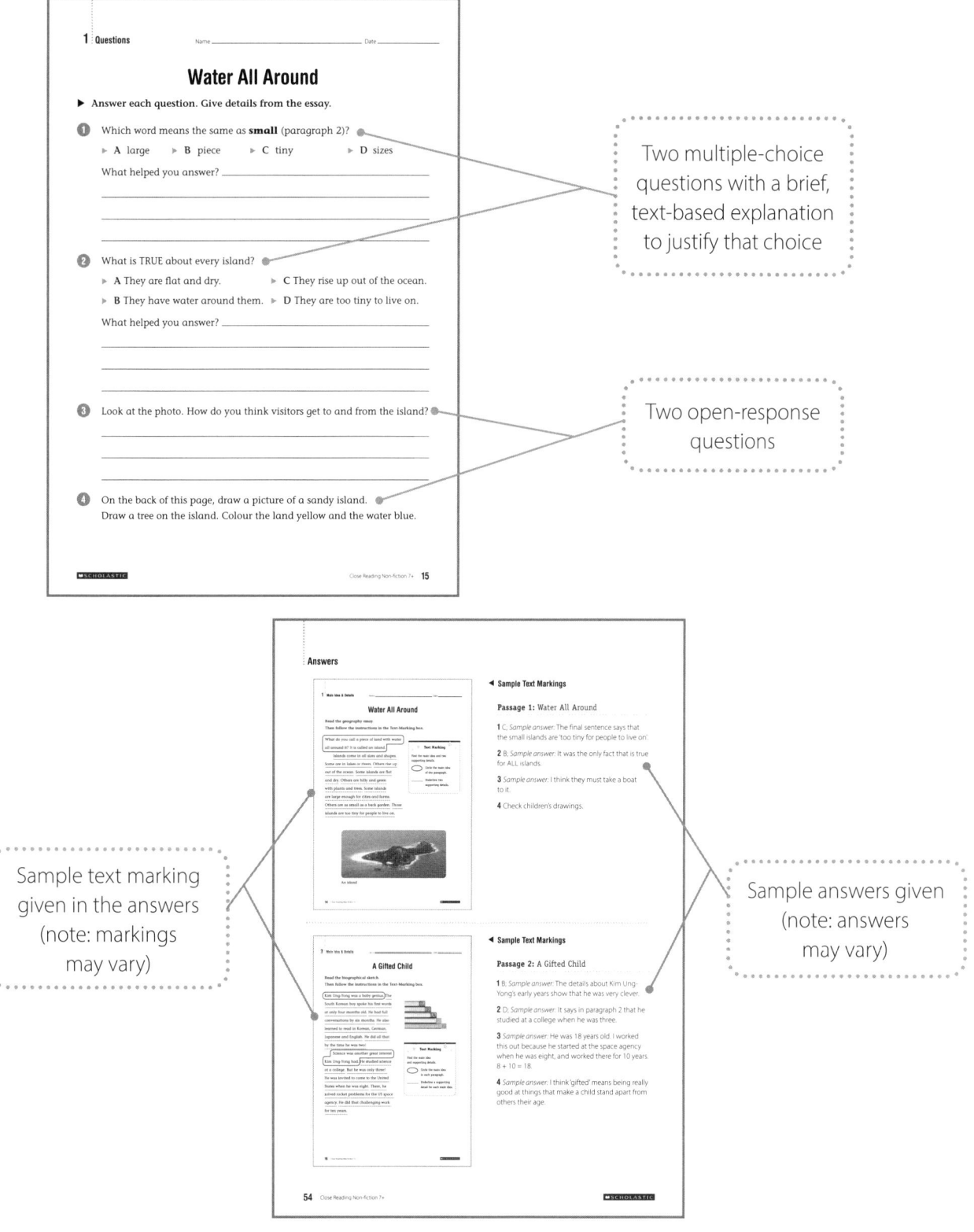

Lexiles

The Lexile Framework® finds the right books for children by measuring readers and texts on the same scale. Lexile measures are the global standard in reading assessment and are accurate for all ages, including first- and second-language learners. The Lexile scores fall within the ranges recommended for children aged 7+.

Introduction

Comprehension Skill Summary Cards

Comprehension Skill Summary Cards are provided on pages 10–13 to help support the children. The terms in bold are the same ones the children will identify as they mark the text.

Give children the relevant card before providing them with the text passage. Discuss the skill together to ensure that children understand it. Encourage the children to use the cards as a set of reading aids to refer to whenever they read any type of fiction text or display the cards in your classroom.

Tips and Suggestions

- The text-marking process is adaptable. While numbering, boxing, circling and underlining are the most common methods, you can personalise the strategy for your class. You might ask the children to use letters to mark text; for example, write MI to indicate a main idea, D to mark a detail, or F for fact and O for opinion.

- You may wish to extend the text-marking strategy by asking the children to identify other aspects of writing, such as confusing words, expressions or idioms.

National Curriculum Correlation

	Passages
• listening to and discussing a wide range of non-fiction	1–20
• reading books that are structured in different ways and reading for a range of purposes	1–20
• checking that the text makes sense to them, discussing their understanding and explaining the meaning of words in context	1, 2, 3, 4, 7, 10, 11, 14, 15, 16, 17, 18, 19
• drawing inferences such as inferring characters' feelings, thoughts and motives from their actions, and justifying inferences with evidence	2, 6, 14, 15, 16, 18
• identifying main ideas drawn from more than one paragraph and summarising these	1, 2, 3, 19, 20
• identifying how language, structure, and presentation contribute to meaning	4, 5, 6, 7, 8
• retrieve and record information from non-fiction	1–20

Teaching Routine for Close Reading and Text Marking

Here is one suggested routine to use Close Reading and Text Marking in the classroom.

Preview

- **Engage prior knowledge** of the passage topic and its genre. Help children link it to similar topics or examples of the genre they may have read.
- **Identify the reading skill** for which children will be marking the text. Display or distribute the relevant Comprehension Skill Summary Card and review these together. (See Comprehension Skill Summary Cards, page 8.)

Model *(for the first passage, to familiarise children with the process)*

- **Display the passage** and provide children with their own copy. Look at the text together by reading the title and looking at the illustration.
- **Draw attention to the markings** children will use to enhance their understanding of the passage. Link the text-marking box to the Comprehension Skill Summary Card for clarification.
- **Read aloud the passage** as children follow along. Guide children to think about the featured skill and to note any questions they may have on sticky notes.
- **Mark the text together.** Begin by numbering the paragraphs. Then discuss the choices you make when marking the text, demonstrating and explaining how various text elements support the skill. Check that children understand how to mark the text using the icons and graphics shown in the text-marking box.

Read

- **Display each passage for a shared reading experience.** Do a quick read of the passage together to familiarise the children with it. Then read it together a second time, pausing as necessary to answer questions, draw connections or clarify words. Then read the passage once more, this time with an eye to the features described in the text-marking box.
- **Invite children to offer ideas for additional markings.** These might include noting unfamiliar vocabulary, an idiom or phrase they may not understand, or an especially interesting, unusual or important detail they want to remember. Model how to use sticky notes, coloured pencils, highlighters or question marks.

Respond

- **If children are able, ask them to read the passage independently.** This reading is intended to allow children to mark the text themselves, with your support, as needed. It will also prepare them to discuss the passage and offer their views about it.
- **Ask the children to answer the questions on the companion questions page.** Depending on the abilities of your children, you might read aloud the questions and then have them answer orally. Model how to look back at the text markings and other text evidence for assistance. This will help children provide complete and supported responses.

Comprehension Skill

Sequence of Events

When you read, look for the **order** in which things happen.

- **Events** are actions or things that happen.

- The **sequence** is the **order** in which events happen.

- **Signal words** give clues about the **sequence of events**.
  Examples: **first, second, next, then, now, later, after, last** and **finally**.

Comprehension Skill

Main Idea & Details

You read to find out things. Some things are more important than others.

- The **main idea** answers 'Who (or What) is this about?'

- The **main idea** is the most important point in the paragraph. Look for a sentence that tells the main idea.

- **Details** add facts about the main idea. Details tell more about the main idea.

Comprehension Skill

Compare & Contrast

When you read, think about how people, things or ideas are alike. Also think about how they are different.

- To **compare** means to tell how things are the same or alike.
- To **contrast** means to tell how things are different.
- **Signal words** give clues that help you compare and contrast.

Examples for comparing: **both, too, like, also** and **in the same way.**

Examples for contrasting: **but, only, however, unlike** and **different.**

Comprehension Skill

Fact & Opinion

When you read, try to spot and separate facts from opinions.

- A **fact** is a statement you can prove. Facts are true.
- An **opinion** tells what someone believes or feels. Opinions vary because people have different beliefs or feelings.
- **Signal words** give clues that help you tell facts from opinions.

Examples for facts: **proof, know** and **found out.**

Examples for opinions: **believe, wish, like, agree, disagree, think, love** and **feel.**

Comprehension Skill

Context Clues

When you read, you may come to words you don't know. Other words nearby may help. Look for words that mean the same or opposite. Or use details to help you work out the meaning.

- **Context** means all the words and sentences around an unknown word.

- **Context clues** are hints that can help you work out the meaning of an unknown word.

Comprehension Skill

Cause & Effect

When you read, think about why something happens. Also think about what happens because of it.

- A **cause** is why something happens.

- An **effect** is what happens.

- If you know the **cause**, try to understand the **effect**.

- If you know the **effect**, try to work out the **cause**.

- **Signal words** give clues that link a cause and its effect.

- Examples: **because, since, so that, in order to** and **as a result.**

Comprehension Skill

Summarise

To summarise what you have read, tell the topic or key idea and details in your own words.

- The **topic** is what you read about.

- Important **details** add more information.

- A **summary** should be short and clear. It should give only the most important details.

Comprehension Skill

Problem & Solution

Sometimes you will read about problems and how they get fixed.

- A **problem** is a kind of trouble or puzzle. A problem needs to be fixed or solved.

- A **solution** is how to solve a problem. A solution makes things better.

- **Signal words** are clues to a problem and its solutions.

Examples for problems: **question**, **need** and **trouble**.

Examples for solutions: **answer**, **idea**, **plan**, **fix**, **result** and **solve**.

1 Main Idea & Details

Name _____ Date _____

Water All Around

Read the geography essay.
Then follow the instructions in the Text-Marking box.

What do you call a piece of land with water all around it? It is called an island.

Islands come in all sizes and shapes. Some are in lakes or rivers. Others rise up out of the ocean. Some islands are flat and dry. Others are hilly and green with plants and trees. Some islands are large enough for cities and farms. Others are as small as a back garden. Those islands are too tiny for people to live on.

Text Marking

Find the main idea and two supporting details.

◯ Circle the main idea of the paragraph.

___ Underline two supporting details.

An island

1 **Questions**   Name _____ Date _____

Water All Around

▶ Answer each question. Give details from the essay.

1 Which word means the same as **small** (paragraph 2)?

▶ **A** large   ▶ **B** piece   ▶ **C** tiny   ▶ **D** sizes

What helped you answer? _____

_____

_____

2 What is TRUE about every island?

▶ **A** They are flat and dry.   ▶ **C** They rise up out of the ocean.

▶ **B** They have water around them.   ▶ **D** They are too tiny to live on.

What helped you answer? _____

_____

_____

3 Look at the photo. How do you think visitors get to and from the island?

_____

_____

_____

4 On the back of this page, draw a picture of a sandy island. Draw a tree on the island. Colour the land yellow and the water blue.

2 Main Idea & Details

Name _____ Date _____

A Gifted Child

**Read the biographical sketch.
Then follow the instructions in the Text-Marking box.**

Kim Ung-Yong was a baby genius. The South Korean boy spoke his first words at only four months old. He had full conversations by six months. He also learned to read in Korean, German, Japanese and English. He did all that by the time he was two!

Science was another great interest Kim Ung-Yong had. He studied science at a college. But he was only three! He was invited to come to the United States when he was eight. There, he solved rocket problems for the US space agency. He did that challenging work for ten years.

Text Marking

Find the main idea and supporting details.

 Circle the main idea in each paragraph.

_____ Underline a supporting detail for each main idea.

2 Questions

Name _____ Date _____

A Gifted Child

▶ Answer each question. Give details from the biographical sketch.

1 A person who is a **genius** (paragraph 1) is very _____.

▶ **A** young   ▶ **B** clever   ▶ **C** active   ▶ **D** helpful

What helped you answer? _____

_____

_____

2 At what age did Kim Ung-Yong begin to study at college?

▶ **A** four months   ▶ **B** six months   ▶ **C** two years   ▶ **D** three years

What helped you answer? _____

_____

_____

3 How old was Kim Ung-Yong when he left his job at the space agency? Explain how you got your answer.

_____

_____

_____

4 What do you think it means for a child to be **gifted**?

_____

_____

_____

_____

Close Reading Non-fiction 7+ **17**

3 Main Idea & Details

No Teeth? No Problem!

Read the nature article.
Then follow the instructions in the Text-Marking box.

The giant anteater has a perfect name. It's very big and it eats ants – thousands of them a day. And it doesn't even have teeth!

This animal's head fits its needs. It has a keen sense of smell. It sniffs out an anthill with its powerful nose. Then it uses its sharp claws to open a hole in the anthill. Now its long, wormlike tongue gets busy. The anteater pokes its tongue deep into the hole. Ants stick to it. The anteater snaps its tongue back into its mouth. It scrapes the ants off and swallows them whole.

But feeding like this isn't easy. Ants sting the tongue. So the anteater must stop to rest it after a minute or so. It goes back later for more, after its tongue stops hurting.

Text Marking

Find the main idea and supporting details.

◯ Circle the main idea in each paragraph.

___ Underline supporting details for each main idea.

A giant anteater

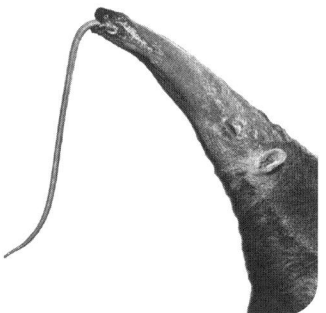
Its long tongue

3 Questions

No Teeth? No Problem!

▶ Answer each question. Give details from the article.

1 Which is the most important topic of the article?

▶ **A** living without teeth ▶ **C** kinds of tongues

▶ **B** insects that sting ▶ **D** giant anteaters

What helped you answer? _____

_____

2 The author says that the giant anteater has a **keen** sense of smell (paragraph 2). Which word means about the same as **keen**?

▶ **A** weak ▶ **B** strong ▶ **C** unusual ▶ **D** surprising

What in the text helped you answer? _____

_____

3 Why does the author say that the giant anteater has a perfect name?

_____

_____

4 Look at the picture of the giant anteater. How do its body parts help it get food?

_____

_____

_____

Close Reading Non-fiction 7+ **19**

4 Sequence of Events

Name _____ Date _____

A New Book

Read the article about books.
Then follow the instructions in the Text-Marking box.

It's your birthday and gifts are waiting to be opened! You happily unwrap one. It's that new book about whales. You are delighted. You hold it up and pause. You remember what your teacher said about how to explore a book before you read it.

    First, study the front and back covers. Read the title and the name of the author. Look at any pictures. Then, flip through the pages to see how they look. Look at the illustrations. Do any grab your attention? Next, turn to the beginning pages of the book to see what's there. Has the author written an introduction? Finally, scan the table of contents. What topics will you read about?

    So, will you open another gift or will you start reading?

Reading a new book

Text Marking

Find the sequence of steps for exploring a book.

☐ Draw boxes around the signal words: **first**, **then**, **next** and **finally**.

____ Underline the important steps.

1-2-3-4 Number the steps for exploring a book in paragraph 2.

4 Questions   Name _____ Date _____

A New Book

▶ Answer each question. Give details from the article.

1 Which is another word for **illustrations** (paragraph 2)?

▶ **A** gifts   ▶ **B** pages   ▶ **C** whales   ▶ **D** pictures

What helped you answer? _____

_____

2 What does the author say is the second thing to do when you explore a new book?

▶ **A** Study the covers.   ▶ **C** Check for an introduction.

▶ **B** Flip through the pages.   ▶ **D** Look at the table of contents.

What helped you answer? _____

_____

3 According to the article, what can you learn from a table of contents?

_____

_____

4 How does the table of contents help you explore a book before you read it?

_____

_____

5 Sequence of Events

Red, White and Blue

Read the cooking article.
Then follow the instructions in the Text-Marking box.

Most children enjoy a healthy snack when they get home from school. Here is an idea for an easy snack you can make yourself. It tastes sweet and creamy. And it has the colours of the Union Jack.

    First, tear a pita bread in half. Now, gently open up the pocket of each half. After that, spread some cream cheese inside. You don't need to cover the whole inside. Use enough cream cheese so that the white shows.

    Next, press some blueberries and strawberry slices into the pita pocket. You can make a pattern with the fruit. Or you can just tuck it in so it fits.

    Good job! Enjoy your colourful snack.

Which step is shown here?

Text Marking

Find the sequence of steps for making a pita snack.

☐   Draw boxes around the signal words: **first**, **now**, **after** and **next**.

_____   Underline the important steps.

1-2-3-4   Number the steps in order.

5 Questions   Name _____ Date _____

Red, White and Blue

▶ Answer each question. Give details from the article.

1 Why does the title go with this article?

   ▶ A Many snacks come in those colours.

   ▶ B Those are the main colours of the snack.

   ▶ C Those are the author's favourite colours.

   ▶ D There is no way to tell.

   What helped you answer? _____

   _____

2 What is the first step the author tells you to do?

   ▶ A Enjoy a snack.   ▶ C Tear a pita bread in half.

   ▶ B Spread cream cheese.   ▶ D Look at a Union Jack.

   What helped you answer? _____

   _____

3 For which step does the author say you can make a pattern? Explain.

   _____

   _____

4 Look at the photo. What should happen next?

   _____

   _____

Close Reading Non-fiction 7+   **23**

6 Sequence of Events

Name _____ Date _____

Teach a Dog a Trick

Read the training article.
Then follow the instructions in the Text-Marking box.

You want to teach your dog to lie down on the floor. Your dog book has a plan you are going to try.

Your dog is sitting down looking at you. That's because you are holding a treat in your hand. Here's what the book says to do.

First, hold the treat near your dog's nose so he or she can smell it. This makes the dog very interested. Now say, "Down" as you move the treat straight down towards the floor. Most dogs really want that treat, so they will follow it. Next, pull the treat towards you along the floor.

When your pet finally lies down all the way, you reward it with the treat.

It's good to practise like this every day.

Good dog!

Text Marking

Find the sequence of steps for training a dog to lie down.

☐ Draw boxes around the signal words.

___ Underline the important steps.

1-2-3-4 Number the steps in order.

6 Questions

Name _____ Date _____

Teach a Dog a Trick

▶ Answer each question. Give details from the article.

1 Which step gets the dog to lie all the way down?

- ▶ **A** pulling the treat towards you along the floor
- ▶ **B** holding the treat in your hand
- ▶ **C** giving the dog the treat
- ▶ **D** having the dog sit

What helped you answer? _____

_____

2 You would say "Good dog!" when _____.

- ▶ **A** the dog first sits
- ▶ **C** it lies all the way down
- ▶ **B** you show it the treat
- ▶ **D** it starts to follow the treat

What helped you answer? _____

_____

3 Why do you use a treat to train a dog?

_____

_____

4 How did the dog owner know what to do to train the dog to lie down?

_____

_____

7 Fact & Opinion

About a Film

Read the film review.
Then follow the instructions in the Text-Marking box.

My parents just took me to see *Frozen*. This cartoon film was made in 2013. It is about two princesses. One is Elsa, and she has magical powers. She uses them to keep the kingdom cold. It is always winter there.

Elsa's sister is Anna. She wants to break the icy spell. So Anna joins up with a mountain man named Kristoff, his reindeer Sven and a snowman called Olaf. They go on a long, dangerous journey to save the land. They face scary wolves, a snow monster and a terrible storm.

I think that this film is perfect for children of all ages. It is both sad and happy and has great characters. Plus, I really liked the ending. I believe that you will love this thrilling film!

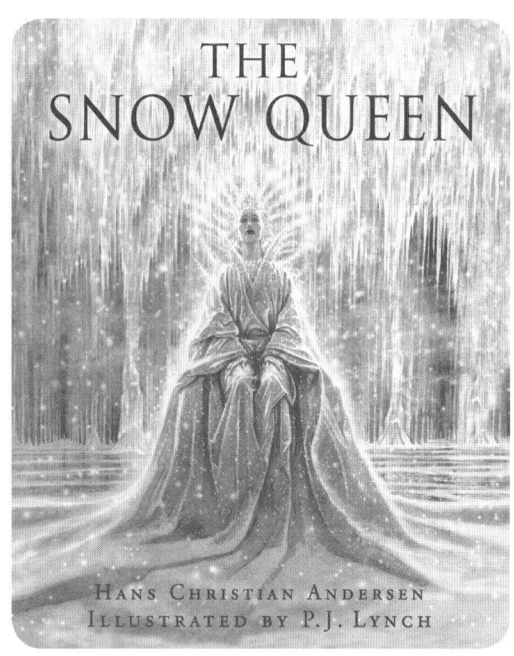

The book that the film *Frozen* was based on

Text Marking

Identify the facts and opinions in the film review.

☐ Draw boxes around the signal words: **I think** and **I believe**.

◯ Circle one fact.

___ Underline one opinion.

26 Close Reading Non-fiction 7+

7 Questions

Name _____ Date _____

About a Film

▶ Answer each question. Give details from the film review.

1 Which of the words below means the same as **thrilling** (paragraph 3)?

▶ **A** cold ▶ **B** long ▶ **C** magical ▶ **D** exciting

What helped you answer? _____

_____

_____

2 Who freezes the kingdom in *Frozen*?

▶ **A** Anna ▶ **B** Elsa ▶ **C** Olaf ▶ **D** Sven

What helped you answer? _____

_____

_____

3 What did the reviewer like about the film?

_____

_____

_____

_____

4 What do phrases like **I think** and **I believe** tell you?

_____

_____

_____

_____

8 Fact & Opinion

Fajitas

Read the food essay.
Then follow the instructions in the Text-Marking box.

The Spanish word *fajitas* (fa-HEE-tas) originally meant 'beef strips'. But for most of us, it names a popular food. Fajitas come from Mexico.

A fajita starts with a flour tortilla (tor-TEE-uh). This round, flat bread may be grilled or steamed. The tortilla is then wrapped around a filling. In my opinion, a fajita is the yummiest food ever.

Many fajitas are filled with meat or beans. But some have other fillings. They might have rice, chicken or fish. Or they might have lettuce, salsa, cheese or soured cream. I like all those things. So, I think that the more ingredients stuffed inside, the better a fajita tastes.

I have made myself hungry! How about you?

Fajitas

Text Marking

Identify the facts and opinions in the essay.

☐ Draw boxes around the signal words: **In my opinion**, **I like** and **I think**.

◯ Circle two facts.

___ Underline two opinions.

8 Questions Name _____ Date _____

Fajitas

▶ Answer each question. Give details from the essay.

1 Which is an ingredient you could find in a fajita?

▶ **A** milk   ▶ **B** steam   ▶ **C** chicken   ▶ **D** grill

What helped you answer? _____

_____

_____

2 What is a tortilla made of?

▶ **A** fish   ▶ **B** flour   ▶ **C** cheese   ▶ **D** lettuce

What helped you answer? _____

_____

_____

3 In the author's view, what makes the best fajita?

_____

_____

_____

4 In what way are ALL fajitas alike?

_____

_____

_____

9 Fact & Opinion

Help Our Playgrounds

Read the letter to the editor.
Then follow the instructions in the Text-Marking box.

To the Editor,

I think our playgrounds are amazing. They help children enjoy fresh air, friends and fun. But not all are safe. I believe it is very important to make them so.

Playground with a rubber surface

    Firstly, playgrounds must have safer surfaces than hard concrete. That is because falls are the most common playground accidents. Rubber or sand are good choices. We should also repair broken equipment to avoid danger.

Text Marking

Identify the facts and opinions in the letter.

☐ Draw boxes around three signal words.

◯ Circle two facts.

__ Underline three opinions.

    But my opinion is that the most important thing to do is to have adults watching all the time. Adults can teach rules for playground safety. No pushing is a good example. Adults can get children to take off scarves or necklaces. That is because these can get caught on equipment. Plus, adults would be there to help if something goes wrong.

    Safety must come first.

Ellie Chang, Inverness

9 Questions

Name _____ Date _____

Help Our Playgrounds

▶ Answer each question. Give details from the letter to the editor.

1 The author talks about repairing 'broken equipment to **avoid** danger' (paragraph 2). When you **avoid** something, you are trying to _____.

- ▶ A keep away from it
- ▶ C make it safer
- ▶ B make it happen
- ▶ D repeat it

What helped you answer? _____

_____

2 Which does the author say causes most playground accidents?

- ▶ A broken equipment
- ▶ C bad weather
- ▶ B wearing scarves
- ▶ D falling

What helped you answer? _____

_____

3 Explain the author's opinion of pushing.

_____

_____

_____

4 Look back at your markings. What does the author believe is the best way to make playgrounds safer?

_____

_____

_____

Close Reading Non-fiction 7+   **31**

10 Compare & Contrast

Name _____ Date _____

Hamster or Gerbil?

Read the science article.
Then follow the instructions in the Text-Marking box.

At first glance, hamsters and gerbils look alike. Both are soft and adorable rodents. Both make good pets. Can you tell them apart?

   One way is to compare how they look. They can be the same size, but look at their tails. A hamster tail is short and stubby. But a gerbil tail is as long as the rest of its body. Now notice their heads. The hamster's head is round with chubby cheeks. But the gerbil's head is narrow, like a mouse's.

   Or you could compare habits. A gerbil plays all day and sleeps at night. In contrast, a hamster sleeps during the day. Suppose you have one of each. If the sound of little feet running on a wheel wakes you up at night, you can probably blame your hamster.

Hamster

Gerbil

Text Marking

Compare and contrast hamsters and gerbils.

☐ Draw boxes around the signal words: **both**, **but** and **in contrast**.

◯ Circle one way they are alike.

___ Underline one way they are different.

32 Close Reading Non-fiction 7+

10 Questions

Name _____ Date _____

Hamster or Gerbil?

▶ Answer each question. Give details from the article.

1 A **first glance** (paragraph 1) is when you _____ something for the first time.

  ▶ **A** hear   ▶ **B** think   ▶ **C** touch   ▶ **D** look at

  What helped you answer? _____
  _____

2 Which is NOT true about gerbils?

  ▶ **A** Gerbils are rodents.   ▶ **C** Gerbils have long tails.

  ▶ **B** Gerbils play at night.   ▶ **D** Gerbils have narrow heads.

  What helped you answer? _____
  _____

3 Describe two ways that hamsters and gerbils look different.
  _____
  _____
  _____

4 Explain one way that hamsters and gerbils act differently.
  _____
  _____
  _____

11 Compare & Contrast

Name _____ Date _____

Football and Netball

Read the sports article.

Then follow the instructions in the Text-Marking box.

Football and netball are different sports. But the balls they use look alike. They are both round. They are both made of rubber. Both are bigger than cricket balls but smaller than basketballs. Like cricket balls and basketballs, the surfaces of footballs and netballs are made from panels.

However, these two balls differ slightly. A netball is a bit smaller and lighter than a football.

Another difference is the design. Netballs are designed for good grip. The players need to be able to catch them and hold on to them. Footballs are designed to fly through the air well. The players mustn't touch the football with their hands. They need it to be able to aim the ball accurately when they kick it.

Football

Netball

Text Marking

Compare and contrast footballs and netballs.

☐ Draw boxes around the signal words: **both**, **however** and **differ**.

◯ Circle two ways they are alike.

___ Underline two ways they are different.

11 Questions   Name _____ Date _____

Football and Netball

▶ Answer each question. Give details from the article.

1 Which word or words could replace **However** in paragraph 2 without changing the meaning of the sentence?

▶ **A** Also   ▶ **B** But   ▶ **C** In addition   ▶ **D** Whenever

What helped you answer? _____

_____

2 Which is TRUE ONLY for netball?

▶ **A** They are round.   ▶ **C** They are made of rubber.

▶ **B** They have panels.   ▶ **D** They must be easy to hold on to.

What helped you answer? _____

_____

_____

3 Why must footballs fly through the air well? Explain.

_____

_____

_____

4 Look back at your markings. Think about the ideas in the article. Why might people mix up footballs and netballs?

_____

_____

_____

12 Compare & Contrast

Nails and Screws

Read the building essay.
Then follow the instructions in the Text-Marking box.

Are you building a table or putting up a shelf? There are many ways to fasten the parts together. One way is to use nails. Another is to use screws.

Nails and screws are both metal fasteners. They have a sharp point at one end and a 'head' at the other end. Both come in many sizes. Builders use both screws and nails in their work. They pick whichever one is best for the job.

But nails and screws have differences. A nail has a smooth 'body' and a flat head. You use a hammer to pound in a nail. By contrast, the body of a screw has a long ridge winding around it. Screw heads may be flat or dome shaped. They have slots where a screwdriver goes. That tool turns and tightens the screw.

How can you tell which is which?

Text Marking

Compare and contrast nails and screws.

☐ Draw boxes around the signal words.

◯ Circle two ways they are alike.

___ Underline two ways they are different.

12 Questions   Name _____ Date _____

Nails and Screws

▶ Answer each question. Give details from the essay.

1 Which is NOT a way to **fasten** (paragraph 1) building materials together?

▶ **A** Use glue.   ▶ **B** Use nails.   ▶ **C** Use screws.   ▶ **D** Use scissors.

What helped you answer? _____

_____

2 Which is a way that nails and screws are alike?

▶ **A** They cost the same.

▶ **B** Both have one pointed end.

▶ **C** They are both easy to remove.

▶ **D** Each needs a hammer to make it go into something.

What helped you answer? _____

_____

_____

3 Why is there a slot in the head of a screw?

_____

_____

4 Look back at your markings. Think about the ideas in the essay. In your own words, summarise the ways nails and screws are alike and different. Use another sheet of paper.

13 Cause & Effect

A Twitchy Muscle

Read the biology article.
Then follow the instructions in the Text-Marking box.

Most people know how hiccups feel. Your body jumps inside. A 'Hic!' sound pops out of your mouth. The hics repeat, making it hard to speak or be quiet. They can embarrass you.

What is the cause of hiccups? It has to do with a muscle inside your body called the diaphragm (DIE-uh-fram). The diaphragm looks like a rounded dome. It stretches across your chest to help you breathe.

The diaphragm usually works well. It keeps air flowing smoothly in and out of your body. But the diaphragm sometimes gets stuck or irritated and can't work well. It twitches, which interrupts the flow of air. The effect is the hiccups.

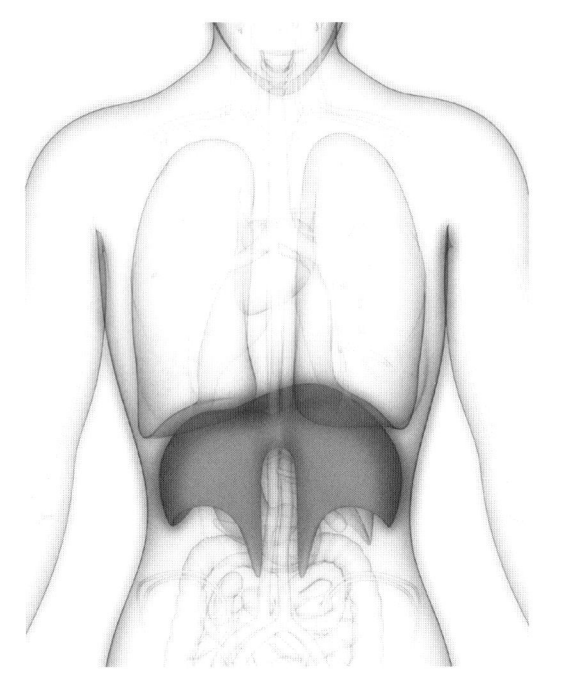

Luckily, hiccups are not serious. They usually go away on their own in a short time.

How the diaphragm looks inside the body

Text Marking

Find the cause and effect.

☐ Draw boxes around the signal words: **cause** and **effect**.

◯ Circle the cause.

___ Underline the effect.

13 Questions

A Twitchy Muscle

▶ Answer each question. Give details from the article.

1 Which is TRUE about hiccups?
- A Hiccups are caused by too much sleep.
- B Hiccups usually go away by themselves.
- C Hiccups are a dangerous health problem.
- D Hiccups help you breathe smoothly.

What helped you answer? _____

_____

2 The **diaphragm** (paragraph 2) is a kind of _____.
- A muscle
- B illness
- C bone
- D sound

What helped you answer? _____

3 What is the main job of the diaphragm in your body?

_____

_____

4 Why do you think some people feel embarrassed by hiccups?

_____

_____

14 Cause & Effect

Name _____ Date _____

Earthquake!

Read the current events article.
Then follow the instructions in the Text-Marking box.

Thousands of fans fill Candlestick Park in San Francisco. A handful of baseball players are on the field. They are stretching, chatting and warming up. The start of Game 3 of the 1989 World Series between the Giants and the Oakland Athletics is moments away. Excitement fills the air.

Suddenly, everything changes. The huge stadium begins to rumble and swing. Lights go out. Cracks form and chunks of concrete fall from the upper stands. Alarmed fans head for the exits. What happened?

What happened is that rock beneath the Earth's surface had suddenly moved. Then the ground began to shake. San Francisco was having a major earthquake!

Bridges buckled and buildings swayed. Highways collapsed. The earthquake caused a halt in the World Series. The games didn't start up again for ten days.

Buildings after the earthquake

Text Marking

Find the cause and effects of the earthquake.

☐ Draw boxes around the signal words.

◯ Circle the cause.

___ Underline the effects.

baseball: a bat-and-ball game a bit like rounders
World Series: an annual baseball competition in North America

40 Close Reading Non-fiction 7+

14 Questions   Name _____ Date _____

Earthquake!

▶ Answer each question. Give details from the article.

1 The word **alarmed** (paragraph 2) probably means _____.

▶ **A** excited   ▶ **B** loud   ▶ **C** afraid   ▶ **D** quiet

What helped you answer? _____
_____

2 Which was NOT an effect of the earthquake?

▶ **A** People lost interest in baseball.   ▶ **C** Game 3 was delayed.

▶ **B** The stadium had to be repaired.   ▶ **D** Bridges had to be fixed.

What helped you answer? _____
_____
_____

3 Why did fans at the stadium want to leave?
_____
_____
_____

4 What makes earthquakes so dangerous?
_____
_____
_____

15 Context Clues

Gyotaku

Read the art history essay.
Then follow the instructions in the Text-Marking box.

Before cameras were invented, Japanese anglers found a clever way to make pictures of the fish they caught. They made fish prints! These prints were known as gyotaku (Ghee-oh-TAK-oo).

Gyotaku is the Japanese word for 'fish printing'.

The process was easy. The anglers used fresh fish, ink and rice paper.

First, the anglers rinsed and dried a fish. They laid it out flat.

Next, they opened out the fins and tail. They fixed them in place with clay or tape. They brushed the fish with ink.

Then, they pressed rice paper against the inked fish. They rubbed the paper from the fish's head to tail. This transferred the ink from the fish on to the paper.

They lifted off the paper and let it dry. The finished pictures were beautiful.

Finally they rinsed the ink off the fish. This made the fish safe to sell or eat!

Text Marking

Use context clues to unlock word meanings.

◯ Circle the words: **anglers** and **transferred**.

___ Underline context clues for each word.

15 Questions Name _____ Date _____

Gyotaku

▶ Answer each question. Give details from the essay.

1 Another word for **anglers** (paragraph 1) is _____.

▶ A artists   ▶ B cameras   ▶ C cleaners   ▶ D fishermen

What helped you answer? _____

_____

2 Why did anglers open out the fish's fins and tails when making a print?

▶ A to get more details in the print   ▶ C to hold the fish still

▶ B to calm the fish down   ▶ D to make the fish easier to clean

What helped you answer? _____

_____

3 What led people to invent the art of fish printing?

_____

_____

4 Some people call *gyotaku* 'transfer printing'. What gets transferred in this art?

_____

_____

16 Context Clues

A Musical Shape

Read the music essay.
Then follow the instructions in the Text-Marking box.

You know that triangles are shapes with three sides. But there is another type of triangle. This other kind is used to make music.

The musical triangle is a steel rod bent into three equal sides. It is a percussion instrument. Like all percussion instruments, triangles must be hit to make music. One corner of the triangle is open. That space allows the instrument to ring clearly.

A player doesn't hold the triangle directly. Hands on the metal would block the sound. Instead, the triangle hangs from a loop made of leather or string. The player holds the loop about chest high to let the triangle float in the air. Triangle players hold a metal bar called a beater in their other hand. They tap this pencil-like object against the triangle to play it. Ring, ring!

Playing a triangle

Text Marking

Use context clues to unlock word meanings.

◯ Circle the words: **percussion**, **instrument** and **beater**.

___ Underline context clues for each word.

16 Questions

A Musical Shape

▶ Answer each question. Give details from the essay.

1 In this essay, the word **instrument** (paragraph 2) is something used to _____.

▶ **A** do maths   ▶ **B** block sound   ▶ **C** make music   ▶ **D** form a loop

What helped you answer? _____

_____

2 Which of these would be another good title for this essay?

▶ **A** Beat It!   ▶ **C** Three Sides of Maths

▶ **B** Girls and Music   ▶ **D** A Percussion Instrument

What helped you answer? _____

_____

3 Why can't triangle players hold their instrument directly?

_____

_____

4 What is true about ALL percussion instruments?

_____

_____

17 Problem & Solution

Name _____ Date _____

Survival Hero

Read the news article.

Then follow the instructions in the Text-Marking box.

Even a child can be a survival hero. Nine-year-old Grayson Wynne was on a family camping trip in the wilderness. He wandered off into the forest. Soon he had a problem – he was lost.

At first, Grayson felt scared. Then he remembered a TV show about survival skills. He looked for a place to shelter. He spent the night under a tree.

Grayson knew he should leave clues to show where he was. The next day he tore up his yellow coat. He tied pieces to the trees. He dropped some bits of paper.

Grayson's solution worked. Many people were searching for him. The clues helped them to find him. Watching TV had saved his life!

Text Marking

Find the problem and its solution.

☐ Draw boxes around the signal words: **problem** and **solution**.

◯ Circle the problem.

___ Underline the solution.

17 Questions   Name _____ Date _____

Survival Hero

▶ Answer each question. Give details from the article.

1 Another word that means the same as **solution** (paragraph 4) is _____.

▶ **A** answer   ▶ **B** hero   ▶ **C** question   ▶ **D** trouble

What helped you answer? _____
_____

2 How did Grayson know what to do to survive and help rescuers to find him?

▶ **A** Grayson's mother was a survival expert.
▶ **B** Grayson had rescued lost people himself.
▶ **C** Grayson had seen what to do on TV.
▶ **D** Grayson had help from another lost person.

What helped you answer? _____
_____

3 What was Grayson's problem? What caused it?
_____
_____
_____

4 Look at the picture. How does it fit the news article?
_____
_____

18 Problem & Solution

Name _____ Date _____

Bad Timing

Read the business letter.
Then follow the instructions in the Text-Marking box.

The owner of a shop got this letter from a young customer.

To William's Watch Shop:

I just bought my first wristwatch at your shop. I used my birthday money to buy it. I picked a My-Time, model WW08, in blue. I know how to tell the time and I really like this watch. But it's not working. It has a brand new battery, so that's not the problem. Something else must be wrong.

My dad suggests two ideas for how you can solve my problem. One solution is for me to return the watch and get my money back. Another plan is for you to let me trade in this watch for another one that works.

Please help me. I hope to hear from you soon.

Yours truly,
Grace Bayley, age 8

Text Marking

Find the problem and its solutions.

☐ Draw boxes around the signal words.

◯ Circle the problem.

___ Underline two solutions.

18 Questions

Bad Timing

▶ Answer each question. Give details from the letter.

1 A **customer** (opening line) of a shop is a person who _____.

▶ A owns it   ▶ B lives there   ▶ C shops there   ▶ D works there

What helped you answer? _____

2 Which best describes Grace's problem?

▶ A She can't tell the time.   ▶ C Her watch cost too much.

▶ B Her watch isn't working.   ▶ D She doesn't like her watch.

What helped you answer? _____

3 Look back at your markings. What solutions does Grace's dad suggest?

4 Why do you think Grace's letter is polite, not angry?

19 Summarise

A Sweets Story

Read the history article.
Then follow the instructions in the Text-Marking box.

An old sweet shop has a new life. America's oldest sweet shop is back.

In 1863, Shane's opened on Market Street in Philadelphia. For many years this sweet shop served tasty treats to happy customers. Shane's was famous for many sweet creations. 'Irish potatoes' were one. These weren't potatoes at all. They were globs of cream cheese mixed with coconut. Cinnamon sprinkled on top made them look brown.

But over time, business fell off. The shop became run down. Then two brothers came to the rescue. Ryan and Eric Berley owned an ice-cream shop nearby. They decided to give Shane's a make-over. They repaired and painted it to look like it once did. They filled its shelves with hundreds of handmade sweets. Hooray for the new Shane's!

Treats available at Shane's

Text Marking

Summarise the text.

◯ Circle the topic.

____ Underline two important details.

19 Questions

A Sweets Story

▶ Answer each question. Give details from the article.

1 When business **falls off** (paragraph 3), it means that a shop gets _____.

- A fewer customers
- B more customers
- C a new life
- D new shelves

What helped you answer? _____

_____

2 **Irish potatoes** were a kind of _____.

- A toy
- B sweet
- C vegetable
- D ice cream

What helped you answer? _____

_____

3 What does it mean for a sweet shop to get **a new life** (paragraph 1)?

_____

_____

4 Look back at your markings. Write a short summary of the main idea of this article. Use another sheet of paper.

20 Summarise   Name _____ Date _____

Hopi *Kachinas*

Read the culture essay.
Then follow the instructions in the Text-Marking box.

The Hopi people of Arizona believe in many gods and spirits. They pay respect to them by carving special dolls out of wood. These painted dolls are called kachinas (kuh-CHEE-nuhz).

Kachinas honour the spirits of animals, such as owls, bears and butterflies. They also honour the spirits of natural objects, like trees, mountains and water.

Kachinas are used to teach Hopi children about their culture. They are also used to ask the spirits for things the Hopi may need. For example, some kachinas are made to ask for good health. Others might be designed to ask for rain or for a good harvest.

Kachinas are dolls. But they are not toys. They are works of fine art created by master artists. Many are on display in museums.

Hopi kachina doll

Text Marking

Summarise the text.

◯ Circle the topic.

___ Underline three important details.

20 Questions Name _____ Date _____

Hopi *Kachinas*

▶ Answer each question. Give details from the essay.

1 Which is NOT true about kachinas?

▶ **A** They are toys.   ▶ **C** They honour spirits.

▶ **B** They are carved.   ▶ **D** They are works of art.

What helped you answer? _____

_____

_____

2 What are kachinas made out of?

▶ **A** animals   ▶ **B** spirits   ▶ **C** wood   ▶ **D** rain

What helped you answer? _____

_____

_____

3 Look at the photo. What animal spirit do you think the artist is showing? Explain.

_____

_____

_____

_____

4 Look back at your markings. Write a short summary of the essay. Explain how Hopi kachinas are used. Use another sheet of paper.

Answers

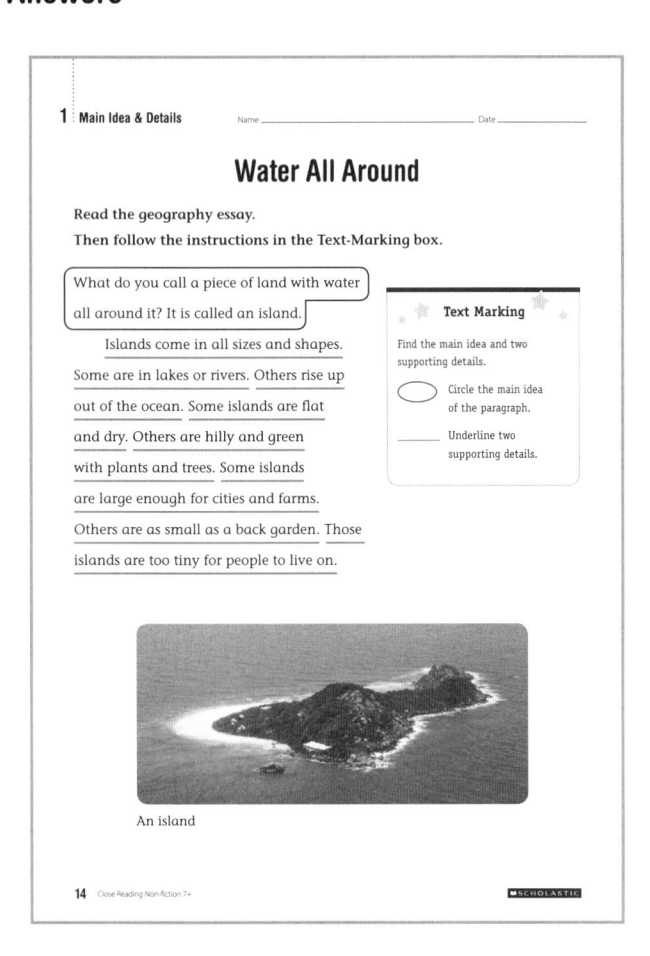

◀ Sample Text Markings

Passage 1: Water All Around

1 C; *Sample answer:* The final sentence says that the small islands are 'too tiny for people to live on'.

2 B; *Sample answer:* It was the only fact that is true for ALL islands.

3 *Sample answer:* I think they must take a boat to it.

4 Check children's drawings.

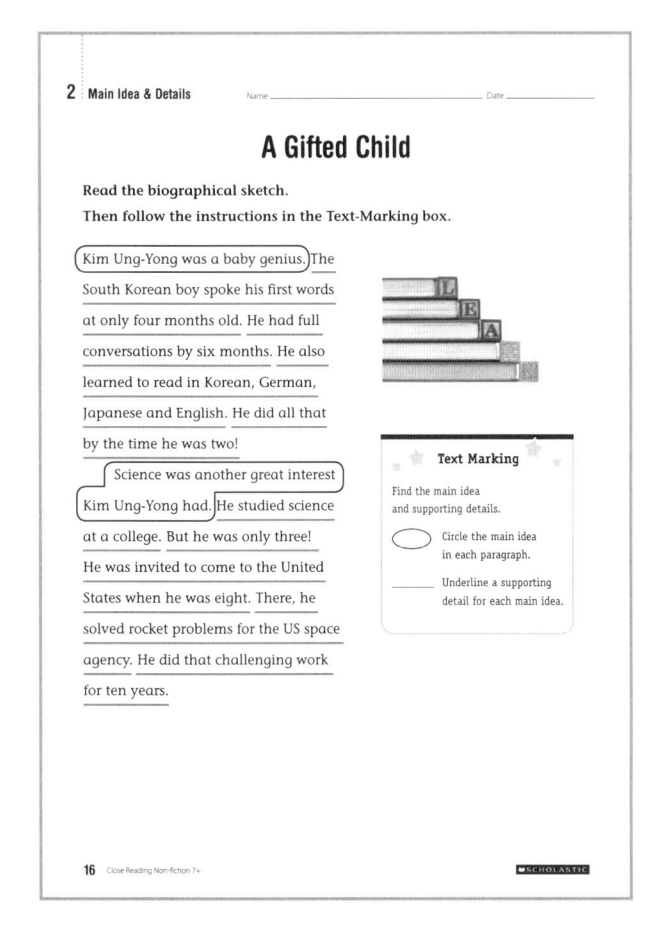

◀ Sample Text Markings

Passage 2: A Gifted Child

1 B; *Sample answer:* The details about Kim Ung-Yong's early years show that he was very clever.

2 D; *Sample answer:* It says in paragraph 2 that he studied at a college when he was three.

3 *Sample answer:* He was 18 years old. I worked this out because he started at the space agency when he was eight, and worked there for 10 years. 8 + 10 = 18.

4 *Sample answer:* I think 'gifted' means being really good at things that make a child stand apart from others their age.

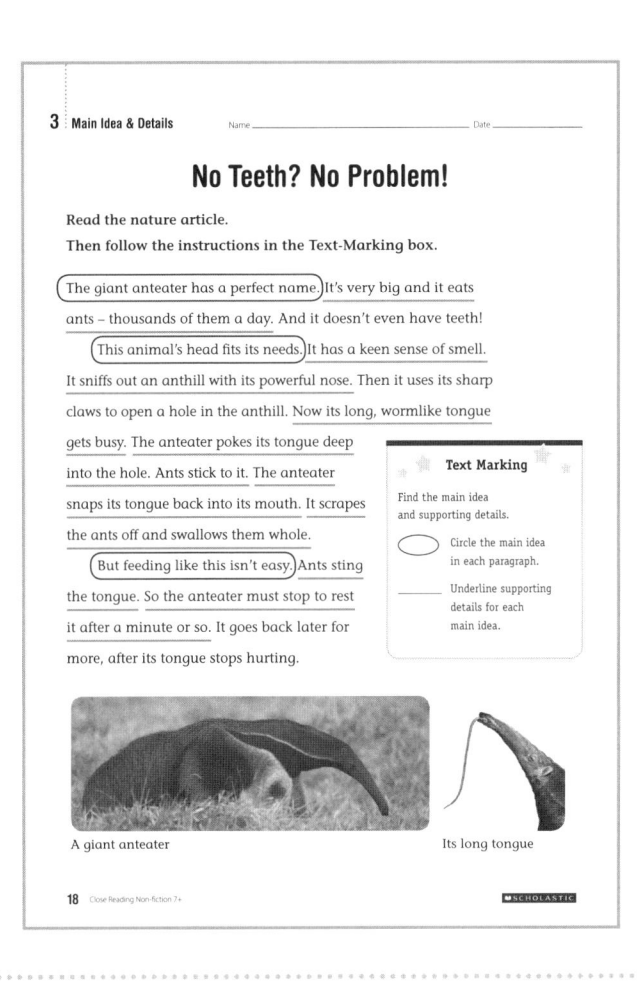

Sample Text Markings

Passage 3: No Teeth? No Problem!

1 D; *Sample answer:* Every paragraph gave information about giant anteaters.

2 B; *Sample answer:* In the next sentence, it says that the anteater has a powerful nose. 'Strong' means about the same thing.

3 *Sample answer:* The name tells exactly what the animal is. It is big and eats ants.

4 *Sample answer:* The long, pointy snout is good for getting into the anthills. The long, sticky tongue helps grab ants.

Sample Text Markings

Passage 4: A New Book

1 D; *Sample answer:* The next sentence asks if they grab your attention so that sounds like it would be pictures. Also, the other answers don't make sense.

2 B; *Sample answer:* In paragraph 2, it's the second thing the author talks about.

3 *Sample answer:* You can learn which topics the author is going to write about in the book.

4 *Sample answer:* It helps give you an idea of what the book is about, what topics are included and if it will be interesting.

Answers

5 Sequence of Events Name Date

Red, White and Blue

Read the cooking article.
Then follow the instructions in the Text-Marking box.

Most children enjoy a healthy snack when they get home from school.
Here is an idea for an easy snack you can make yourself. It tastes sweet and creamy. And it has the colours of the Union Jack.

Which step is shown here?

1 First, tear a pita bread in half. Now,
2 gently open up the pocket of each half.
3 After that, spread some cream cheese inside. You don't need to cover the whole inside. Use enough cream cheese so that the white shows.
4 Next, press some blueberries and strawberry slices into the pita pocket. You can make a pattern with the fruit. Or you can just tuck it in so it fits.

Good job! Enjoy your colourful snack.

Text Marking

Find the sequence of steps for making a pita snack.

☐ Draw boxes around the signal words: **first**, **now**, **after** and **next**.

____ Underline the important steps.

1-2-3-4 Number the steps in order.

22 Close Reading Non-fiction 7+ SCHOLASTIC

◀ Sample Text Markings

Passage 5: Red, White and Blue

1 B; *Sample answer:* The article is all about making a healthy snack with foods that have those colours.

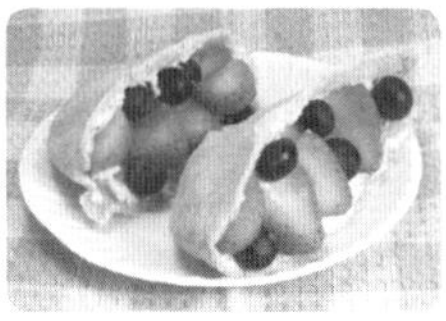

2 C; *Sample answer:* This is what it says after the signal word 'first'.

3 *Sample answer:* Step 4 says you can make a pattern with the fruit, like red/blue, red/blue.

4 *Sample answer:* The picture shows the finished snack. Next you would eat it!

6 Sequence of Events Name Date

Teach a Dog a Trick

Read the training article.
Then follow the instructions in the Text-Marking box.

You want to teach your dog to lie down on the floor. Your dog book has a plan you are going to try.

Your dog is sitting down looking at you. That's because you are holding a treat in your hand. Here's what the book says to do.

Good dog!

1 First, hold the treat near your dog's nose so he or she can smell it. This
2 makes the dog very interested. Now say, "Down" as you move the treat straight down towards the floor. Most dogs really want that treat, so they will follow it.
3 Next, pull the treat towards you along the floor.
4 When your pet finally lies down all the way, you reward it with the treat.

It's good to practise like this every day.

Text Marking

Find the sequence of steps for training a dog to lie down.

☐ Draw boxes around the signal words.

____ Underline the important steps.

1-2-3-4 Number the steps in order.

24 Close Reading Non-fiction 7+ SCHOLASTIC

◀ Sample Text Markings

Passage 6: Teach a Dog a Trick

1 A; *Sample answer:* Trying to reach the treat is what makes the dog lie all the way down.

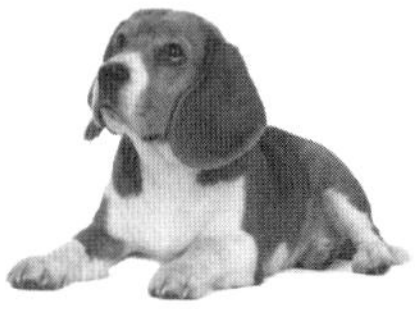

2 C; *Sample answer:* The photo gives me the hint that the dog is a 'good dog' when it has learned to lie down.

3 *Sample answer:* Most dogs love treats, so it makes them interested and gets them to work to learn the trick for a reward.

4 *Sample answer:* It says at the beginning of the article that the dog owner looked it up in a dog book.

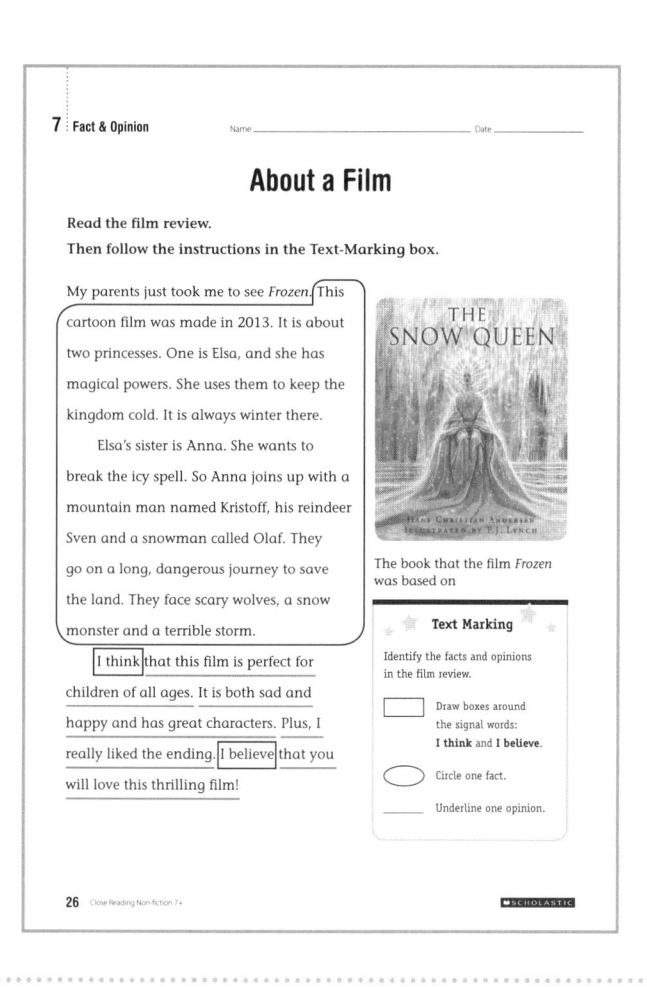

◀ **Sample Text Markings**

Passage 7: About a Film

1 D; *Sample answer:* The author says that this film is about a dangerous journey with a lot of adventures.

2 B; *Sample answer:* In the first paragraph, it says that Elsa keeps the kingdom cold.

3 *Sample answer:* The reviewer liked the characters, the excitement, the happy and sad parts, and the ending.

4 *Sample answer:* These words tell you that the author is giving an opinion.

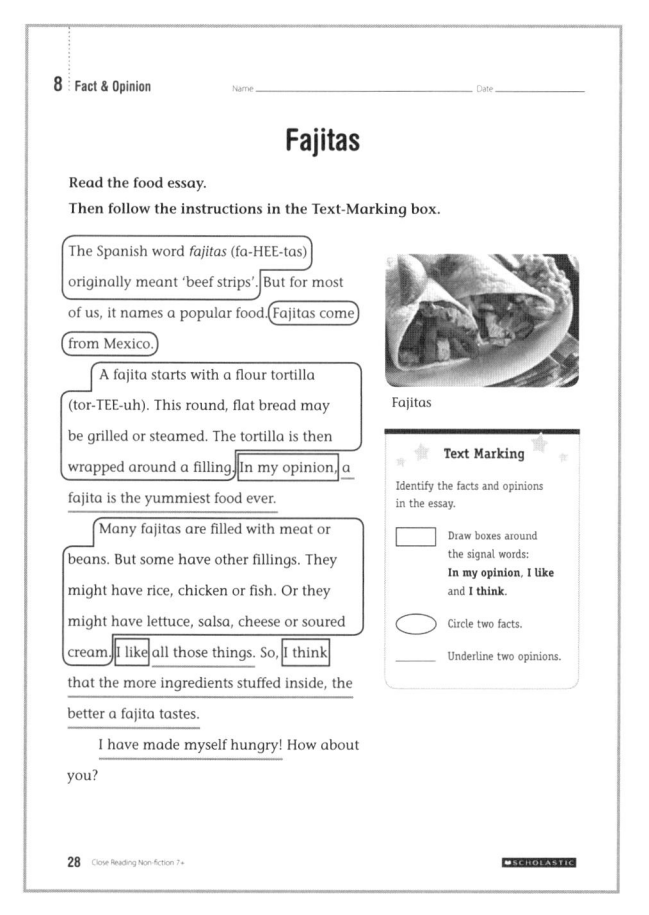

◀ **Sample Text Markings**

Passage 8: Fajitas

1 C; *Sample answer:* Chicken is one of the fillings the author lists in paragraph 3.

2 B; *Sample answer:* It says so in the first sentence of paragraph 2. All the other choices are fillings or toppings.

3 *Sample answer:* Paragraph 3 says that the author likes all the fillings, so the more things inside a fajita, the better the author likes it.

4 *Sample answer:* It says in paragraph 2 that all fajitas are made of flour tortillas that are wrapped around one or more ingredients.

Close Reading Non-fiction 7+ **57**

Answers

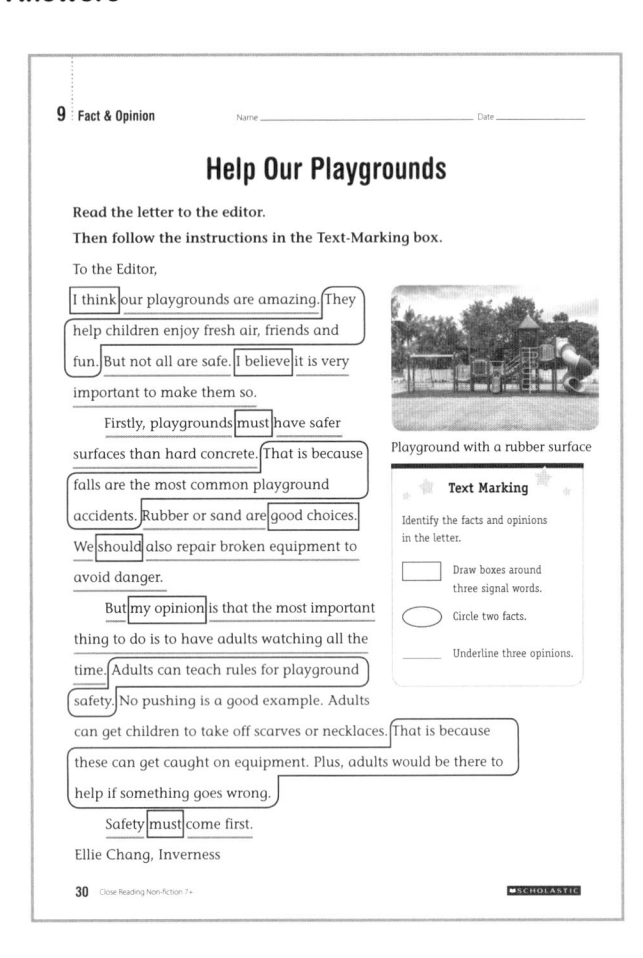

Sample Text Markings

Passage 9: Help Our Playgrounds

1 A; *Sample answer:* Danger is something you want to stay away from.

2 D; *Sample answer:* In paragraph 2, the author says that 'falls are the most common playground accidents'.

3 *Sample answer:* The author is against pushing. I know this because the author gave this as an example of a bad thing that children do that adults can help stop.

4 *Sample answer:* In the last paragraph, the author says that having adults there all the time is the best way to make playgrounds safer.

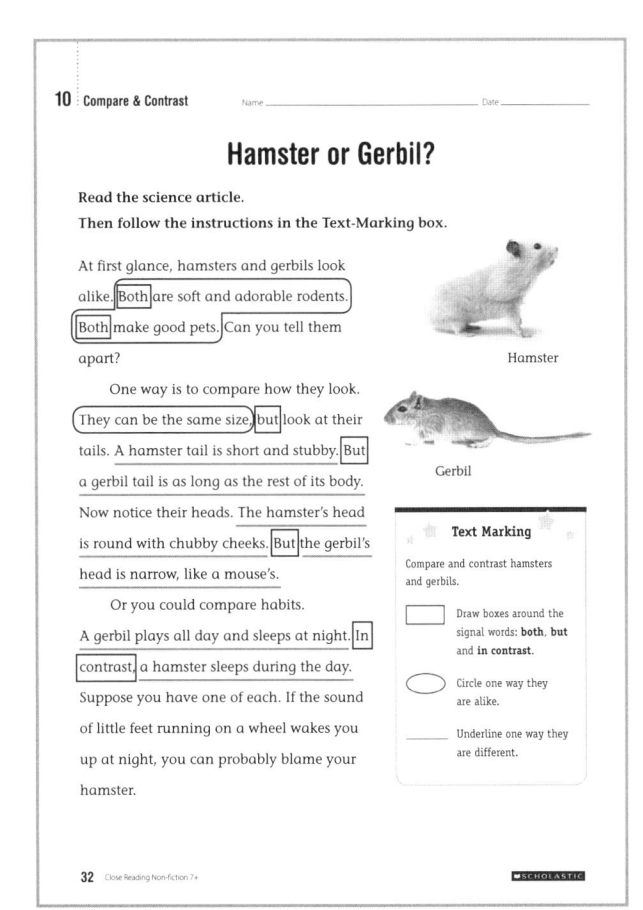

Sample Text Markings

Passage 10: Hamster or Gerbil?

1 D; *Sample answer:* The first paragraph describes what you first see.

2 B; *Sample answer:* In paragraph 3, it says that gerbils play all day and sleep at night.

3 *Sample answer:* Hamsters have short tails but gerbils have long ones. And hamsters have round, chubby faces but gerbils have narrow faces.

4 *Sample answer:* Gerbils sleep at night, but hamsters sleep during the day.

11 Compare & Contrast

Football and Netball

Read the sports article.
Then follow the instructions in the Text-Marking box.

Football and netball are different sports. But the balls they use look alike. They are both round. They are both made of rubber. Both are bigger than cricket balls but smaller than basketballs. Like cricket balls and basketballs, the surfaces of footballs and netballs are made from panels.

However, these two balls differ slightly. A netball is a bit smaller and lighter than a football.

Another difference is the design. Netballs are designed for good grip. The players need to be able to catch them and hold on to them. Footballs are designed to fly through the air well. The players mustn't touch the football with their hands. They need it to be able to aim the ball accurately when they kick it.

Text Marking

Compare and contrast footballs and netballs.

- Draw boxes around the signal words: **both**, **however** and **differ**.
- Circle two ways they are alike.
- Underline two ways they are different.

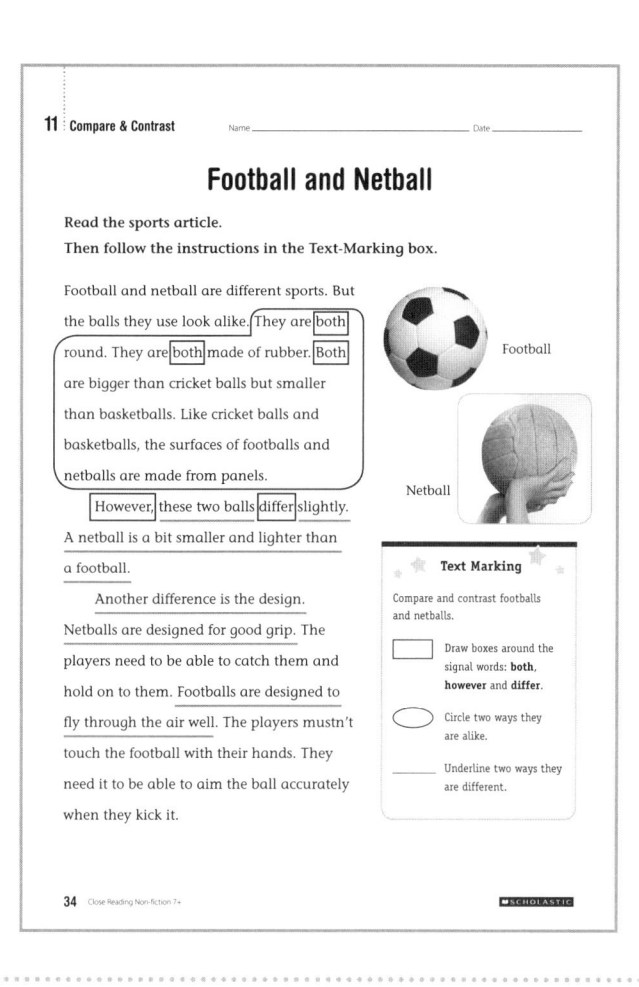

◀ **Sample Text Markings**

Passage 11: Football and Netball

1 B; *Sample answer: But* is the only one that shows contrast.

2 D; *Sample answer:* The other choices are true for netballs and footballs.

3 *Sample answer:* It says in paragraph 3 that footballers need to be able to aim the ball accurately by kicking it. It is important for the ball to fly well so that they can control where it goes.

4 *Sample answer:* Both kinds of balls are made of panels of rubber. Also, people might not notice that netballs are slightly smaller and lighter than footballs.

---

12 Compare & Contrast

Nails and Screws

Read the building essay.
Then follow the instructions in the Text-Marking box.

Are you building a table or putting up a shelf? There are many ways to fasten the parts together. One way is to use nails. Another is to use screws.

Nails and screws are both metal fasteners. They have a sharp point at one end and a 'head' at the other end. Both come in many sizes. Builders use both screws and nails in their work. They pick whichever one is best for the job.

But nails and screws have differences. A nail has a smooth 'body' and a flat head. You use a hammer to pound in a nail. By contrast, the body of a screw has a long ridge winding around it. Screw heads may be flat or dome shaped. They have slots where a screwdriver goes. That tool turns and tightens the screw.

How can you tell which is which?

Text Marking

Compare and contrast nails and screws.

- Draw boxes around the signal words.
- Circle two ways they are alike.
- Underline two ways they are different.

◀ **Sample Text Markings**

Passage 12: Nails and Screws

1 D; *Sample answer:* I know that glue can be used to hold things together but scissors are for cutting, not putting together.

2 B; *Sample answer:* It says in paragraph 2 that nails and screws have a sharp point at one end.

3 *Sample answer:* In paragraph 3, it says a slot is where a screwdriver fits in so you can turn and tighten the screw.

4 *Sample answer:* Both nails and screws can be used to fasten things together. Both are made of metal, come in many sizes and have a point at one end. But they have different kinds of heads, and only screws have ridges.

Answers

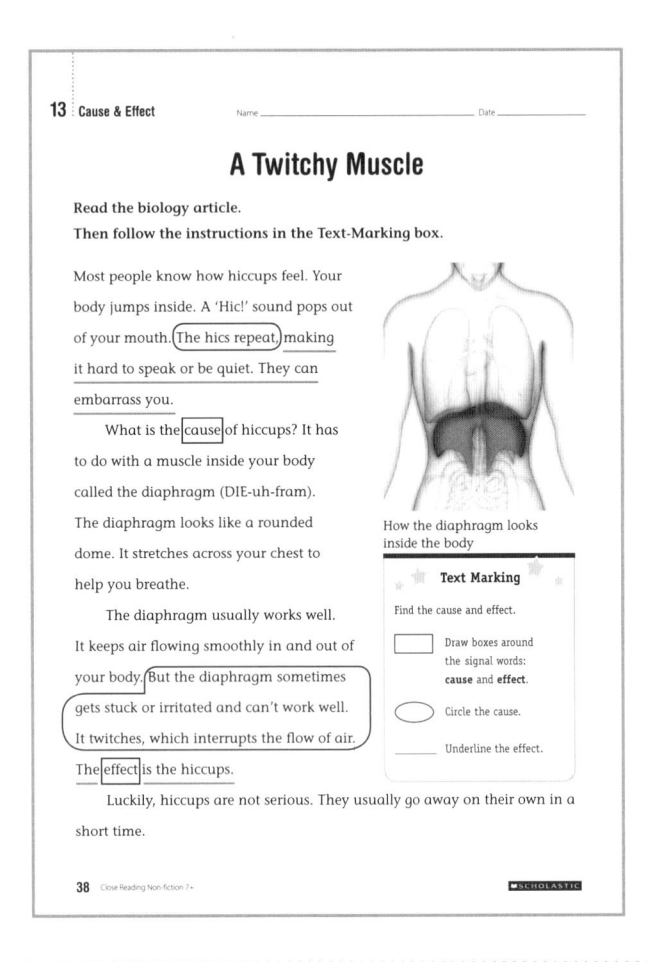

◀ Sample Text Markings

Passage 13: A Twitchy Muscle

1 B; *Sample answer:* It's the only answer that the article talks about.

2 A; *Sample answer:* The second sentence in paragraph 2 says that it is a muscle.

3 *Sample answer:* It says in paragraph 3 that it helps keep air flowing smoothly in and out as you breathe.

4 *Sample answer:* I think that, since hiccups make it hard to speak or keep quiet, some people feel embarrassed. Others might stare or laugh at a person with hiccups.

◀ Sample Text Markings

Passage 14: Earthquake!

1 C; *Sample answer:* The earthquake was scary, so 'afraid' is the best answer.

2 A; *Sample answer:* The article says that the stadium was damaged and bridges buckled, so they needed to be repaired. Also, the last paragraph says that the World Series didn't start up again for ten days, so game 3 was delayed. But I don't think people lost interest in baseball.

3 *Sample answer:* They were afraid of getting hurt or trapped and wanted to get away from the danger.

4 *Sample answer:* When the earth rumbles and moves, it can cause a lot of damage to buildings, streets and bridges. People can get hurt or worse.

◀ Sample Text Markings

Passage 15: *Gyotaku*

1 D; *Sample answer:* Later in the sentence that uses this word, it says 'fish they caught'.

2 A; *Sample answer:* A makes the most sense. If the fins and tail weren't opened out, they might not show up clearly.

3 *Sample answer:* Fishermen wanted pictures of the fish they caught, but they didn't have cameras then.

4 *Sample answer:* The image of the fish. By rubbing the fish on the paper, the ink from the fish is transferred to the paper.

◀ Sample Text Markings

Passage 16: A Musical Shape

1 C; *Sample answer:* The essay tells about a triangle, an instrument that makes music.

2 D; *Sample answer:* D is the only choice that gets at the main idea of the essay.

3 *Sample answer:* If the player holds the triangle by one of its sides, the sound will get blocked.

4 *Sample answer:* It says in paragraph 2 that all percussion instruments make their sounds by being hit.

Answers

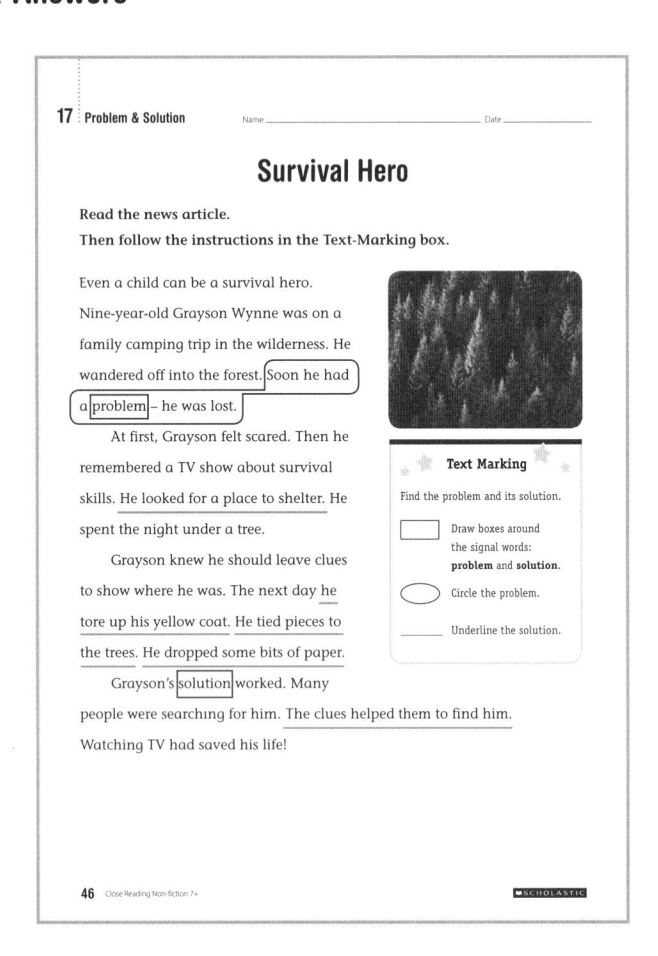

◀ **Sample Text Markings**

Passage 17: Survival Hero

1 A; *Sample answer:* The solution is the answer Grayson came up with to survive in the wilderness.

2 C; *Sample answer:* In paragraph 2 of the article, the author says that Grayson had seen a programme on TV about survival and rescue.

3 *Sample answer:* Grayson's problem was that he was lost in the wilderness. This happened because he wandered away from his family.

4 *Sample answer:* It shows a forest like the one Grayson got lost in and shows how easily it could be to get lost and how difficult it might be to find your way out again.

◀ **Sample Text Markings**

Passage 18: Bad Timing

1 C; *Sample answer:* The letter says Grace Bayley bought her watch at the shop. That means she shopped there.

2 B; *Sample answer:* This is the reason she wrote the letter. She is unhappy that her watch isn't working.

3 *Sample answer:* Her dad suggests Grace returns the watch to get her money back. Or she could trade in the watch for another one that does work.

4 *Sample answer:* Maybe Grace thinks it's better to be nice so the people at the shop will want to help her.

◀ Sample Text Markings

Passage 19: A Sweets Story

1 A; *Sample answer:* I think this is what happened to Shane's. People stopped coming and the shop was no longer busy. Then it got run down.

2 B; *Sample answer:* The author says that Irish Potatoes are sweets made of cream cheese, coconut and cinnamon.

3 *Sample answer:* I think it means that the old, rundown shop was renovated and became popular again.

4 *Sample answer:* This article is about how two brothers fixed up a famous, old sweet shop to make it look like it used to so customers would come back.

◀ Sample Text Markings

Passage 20: Hopi *Kachinas*

1 A; *Sample answer:* In the last paragraph, the author says that kachinas are dolls but are not toys.

2 C; *Sample answer:* The essay says kachinas are carved from wood.

3 *Sample answer:* I think this kachina shows a kind of bird, maybe an owl. I see it has feathers and big eyes, but a person's body.

4 *Sample answer:* The essay is about kachinas, wooden dolls that are carved by the Hopi people. They are used to teach Hopi culture, to make wishes and to pay respect to Hopi gods and spirits.

Close Reading Non-fiction 7+   **63**

SCHOLASTIC

Available for Lexile Levels BR–1000+

SHORT READS

FICTION AND NON-FICTION

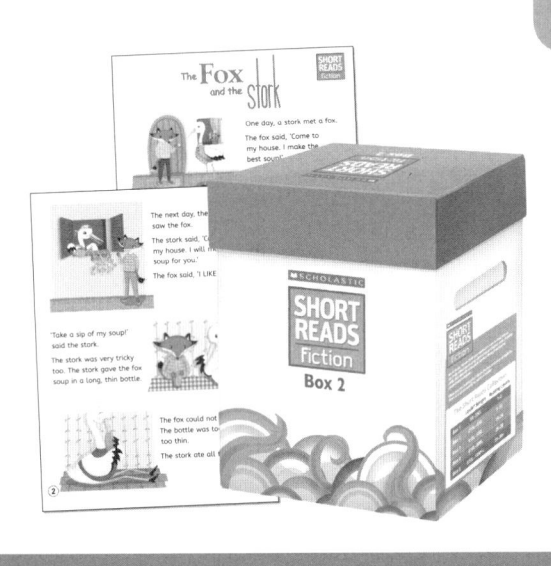

Develop deep comprehension skills with close and repeated reading

✓ Short fiction and non-fiction reading cards for all abilities

✓ Engaging topics and snappy reads across a range of text types

✓ Creative activities for comprehension, peer discussion and writing

✓ Perfect for group reading, pairs or independent reading

✓ Supportive teacher's notes with research-proven techniques

www.scholastic.co.uk/shortreads